FROM CATERPILLAR TO BUTTERFLY

Anita Ganeri

Heinemann Library
Chicago, Illinois

Customer Service 888-454-2279
Visit our website at www.heinemannraintree.com

Designed by Ron Kamen and edesign
Printed and bound in China by South China Printing Company

10 09 08
10 9 8 7 6 5 4 3 2

Library of Congress Cataloging-in-Publication Data
Ganeri, Anita, 1961-
  From caterpillar to butterfly / Anita Ganeri.
      p. cm. -- (How living things grow)
  Includes bibliographical references.
  ISBN 1-4034-7855-4 (library binding - hardcover) -- ISBN 1-4034-7864-3 (pbk.)
  ISBN 978-1-4034-7855-9 (library binding - hardcover) -- ISBN 978-1-4034-7864-1 (pbk.)
  1. Butterflies--Life cycles--Juvenile literature. 2.Caterpillars--Juvenile literature. I. Title. II. Series.
  QL544.2.G35 2006
  595.78'9--dc22
                                    2005026913

Acknowledgments
The author and publishers are grateful to the following for permission to reproduce copyright material: Alamy pp. **9**, **10**, **18**, **19**, **24** (Robert M. Vera), **26**, **27**, **29** (Jill Stephenson); Ardea p. **20** (Francois Gohier); Corbis pp. **6** (George D. Lepp), **29** (Michael & Patricia Fogden); FLPA pp. **11** (S & D & K Maslowski), **13** (Dembinsky Photo Ass.), **14** (Tom and Pam Gardner), **22** (Frans Lanting/Minden Pictures), **23** (Frans Lanting/Minden Pictures); Naturepl.com p. **5** (Tom Vezo); NHPA p. **4** (Stephen Dalton), **12** (Rod Planck), **15** (T Kitchin & V Hurst), **16** (T Kitchin & V Hurst), **17** (T Kitchin & V Hurst), **25** (Stephen Dalton); Oxford Scientific Library p. **7**; Photolibrary.com p. **8**.

Cover photograph of a butterfly reproduced with permission of NHPA/Stephen Dalton.

Illustrations by Martin Sanders

The publishers would like to thank Michael Scott for his assistance in the preparation of this book.

Every effort has been made to contact copyright holders of any material reproduced in this book. Any omissions will be rectified in subsequent printings if notice is given to the publisher.

The paper used to print this book comes from sustainable resources.

Some words are shown in bold, **like this**. You can find out what they mean by looking in the glossary.

Contents

Have You Ever Seen a Butterfly?

Butterflies live all over the world.
There are many kinds of butterflies.
A butterfly is a type of **insect**.

*A butterfly has two pairs of wings, two **antennae**, and three pairs of legs.*

You are going to learn about a monarch butterfly. You will learn how a monarch butterfly is born, grows up, has babies, gets old, and dies. This is the butterfly's life cycle.

How does the butterfly's life cycle start?

Butterfly Eggs

The butterfly starts life as a tiny egg. A female butterfly lays the eggs in the summer. She lays hundreds of eggs on the leaves of a **milkweed** plant.

The female lays her eggs, then she flies away.

*Each egg is about
as big as a grain of rice.*

The little eggs are white and
oval-shaped. They have small
grooves running down the sides.

What happens
to the eggs?

Hungry Caterpillars

About four days later, the eggs start to **hatch**. There is a little **caterpillar** in each egg. The caterpillar chews a hole in its egg.

Squeezing out of the egg is hard work.

The caterpillar is hungry!
First, it eats up its eggshell.
Then, it starts to munch on
the juicy **milkweed** leaves.

The caterpillar spends all day eating.

9

Warning Stripes

A monarch **caterpillar** has yellow, white, and black stripes. They warn birds that the caterpillar is **poisonous**!

These bright colors are hard to miss.

Birds like to eat green caterpillars like this one.
But they keep away from caterpillars with stripes.

The caterpillar gets its poison from
the **milkweed** leaves it eats.
The leaves have a juice in them
that makes the caterpillar
taste bad.

How quickly does the
caterpillar grow?

11

Growing Bigger

The **caterpillar** grows very quickly, but its outer skin does not grow. Soon its skin gets so tight that it splits open and falls off.

The caterpillar is fully grown and ready for the next stage of its life.

The caterpillar has a new, stretchy skin under its old one. It changes its skin this way four or five times as it grows. This is called **molting**.

13

A Tough Case

It is two weeks after the **caterpillar hatched**. Now, it has reached its full size. It hangs upside down from a leaf or twig. Then, its striped skin splits for the last time.

Inside the chrysalis, the caterpillar begins to change.

There is a hard case under this skin. This case is called a **chrysalis**. It is green and gold. The chrysalis keeps the caterpillar safe inside.

How does the caterpillar change into a butterfly?

15

Beautiful Butterfly

The **caterpillar's** body changes inside the **chrysalis**. It turns into a butterfly. This takes about ten days. Then, the chrysalis splits open. A butterfly wriggles out.

It takes the butterfly about an hour to get out of the chrysalis.

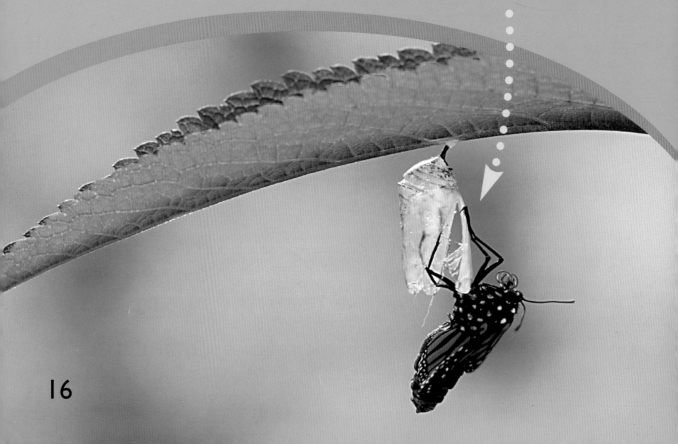

The new butterfly holds its wings out so that they dry.

At first, the butterfly's wings are soft and damp. They soon dry and get hard. The beautiful butterfly is ready to fly away.

What does the butterfly eat?

17

Flower Food

The butterfly eats a sweet juice made by flowers. This juice is called **nectar**.

The butterfly sucks up the nectar with its long tongue. Its tongue works like a drinking straw.

The butterfly's long tongue reaches into the flower.

19

A Long Flight

In the fall, it starts to get colder.
The butterfly cannot stand the cold.
If it gets too cold, it will die. Instead,
it gets ready for a very long flight.

*Millions of butterflies
start their long flight.*

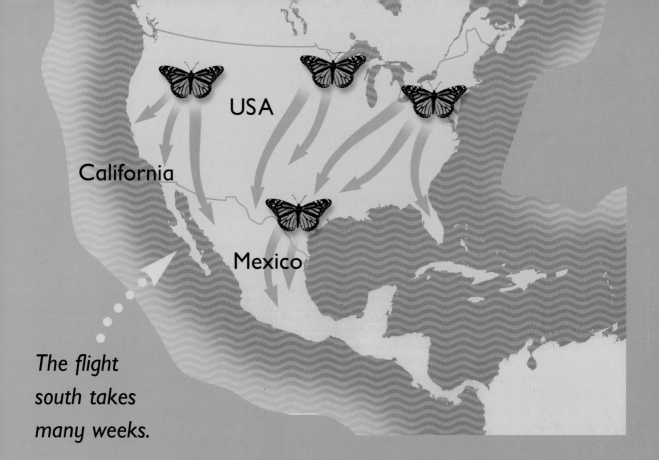

The flight south takes many weeks.

The butterfly flies south to a warmer place. Some butterflies fly to California. Some butterflies fly to Mexico.

What does the butterfly do there?

Winter Sleep

After its long flight, the butterfly lands on a tree. Then, the butterfly goes into a deep sleep for most of the winter. This sleep is called **hibernation**.

Lots of butterflies group together on the branches.

While the butterfly is hibernating, its body works very slowly. This helps it to save **energy**. The butterfly does not eat. It lives off stores of fat in its body.

When does the butterfly wake up?

Waking Up

Spring comes and it gets warmer. The butterfly wakes up from its sleep. It finds some flowers to feed on. Then, the butterfly starts to fly back north.

*The butterfly needs **energy** for the long flight home.*

Some male and female butterflies **mate** on the way. Then, the female lays her eggs. **Caterpillars hatch** and turn into butterflies. These new butterflies also fly north.

Many butterflies die long before they complete their journey north.

What happens to the butterflies?

More Butterflies

When they finish their journey, the butterflies lay more eggs, then they die. The eggs **hatch** into more adult butterflies. These lay more eggs, then they also die.

Some adult butterflies only live for a few weeks.

Butterflies that hatch in spring and summer never have to make the long flight south. Their life cycle begins again in the north.

Life Cycle of a Monarch Butterfly

1 Butterfly **mates** and lays eggs

2 Eggs **hatch**

3 **Caterpillar** feeds and grows

4 Caterpillar inside **chrysalis**

5 Adult butterfly

6 Butterfly feeds on flowers

7 Butterfly flies south in the fall

8 Butterfly hibernates in the winter

9 Butterfly wakes and flies back north in spring

28

Note: Butterflies that hatch in the spring and summer miss out on stages 7, 8, and 9.

Caterpillar Map

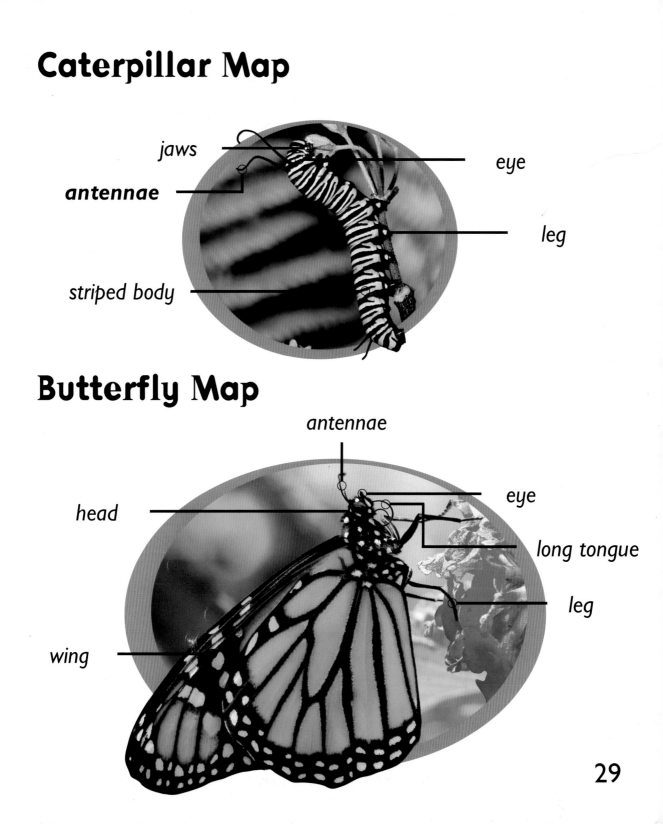

jaws

antennae

eye

leg

striped body

Butterfly Map

antennae

head

eye

long tongue

leg

wing

Glossary

antennae feelers on an insect's head

caterpillar young butterfly that hatches out of an egg

chrysalis hard case that grows around a caterpillar

energy power needed for an animal's body to work

hatch to break out of an egg

hibernation deep sleep during the winter

insect animal with six legs, such as a butterfly

mate when a male and female animal come together to make young

milkweed kind of plant with pink flowers that grows in North America

molting when an animal's old skin falls off and a new skin grows underneath

nectar sweet juice made in a flower

oval-shaped shaped like a circle stretched out on its sides

poisonous full of juice that is bad-tasting or dangerous to eat

More Books to Read

Ganeri, Anita. *Nature's Patterns: Animal Life Cycles.* Chicago: Heinemann Library, 2005.

Parker, Victoria. *Life as a Butterfly.* Chicago: Raintree, 2004.

Rockwell, Anne. *Becoming Butterflies.* New York: Walker, 2002.

Royston, Angela. *Life Cycle of a Butterfly.* Chicago: Heinemann Library, 1998.

Spilsbury, Louise. *Life Cycles: Butterfly.* Chicago: Heinemann Library, 2005.

Waxman, Laura. *Monarch Butterflies.* Minneapolis: Lerner, 2003.

Index